Contents

PRINCIPLES OF CHEMICAL ENGINEERING

A GUIDE TO CHEMICAL ENGINEERING STUDENTS

DR. ADWIN JOSE P

I

CHEMICAL PROCESS INDUSTRIES

CHEMICAL PROCESS INDUSTRIES

INTRODUCTION

Any definition or description of the chemical process industry is always incomplete. Most process in the chemical industry involves a chemical change.

The chemical change includes chemical reactions and physiochemical changes. Mechanical changes are not considered the part of chemical process but it is essential to later chemical changes.

Example: The manufacture of plastic polyethylene using ethylene involves a chemical process. But molding and fabrication of the plastic resin into final shapes for consumer products would not be considered as chemical process.

Some industries which depend on chemical changes are not considered a part of chemical process industry. Because of traditions, special processes, large volume of particular product such as paper or steel.

Example

1. In food industry cheese making involves a fermentation reaction is not considered chemical process industry. But fermentation of sugar to alcohol is listed as chemical industry.
2. The huge metallurgical industry is usually distinguished from chemical process industry because of special nature of the product. But the processing of metals is considered on segment of chemical industry.

Types of chemical Process Industries

1. In organic chemicals industry
2. Organic chemical industry
3. Petrochemical industry
4. Biochemical industry
5. Pulp and paper industry
6. Pigment and paint industry
7. Rubber, Fiber and plastic industry
8. Mineral industry
9. Metal industry

ROLE OF CHEMICAL PROCESS INDUSTRIES IN SOCIETY

- Products of the chemical process industries are used in all areas of everyday life.

- Automobile tires, footwear and electrical insulations are synthesized from natural rubber or synthetic rubber, which is synthesized in chemical process rubber industries.
- The raising of food plants and animals requires chemical fertilizers, insecticides and disinfectants which are manufactured in Biochemical process industries.
- Many building materials have been chemically processed. Example-Metals, concretes, roofing materials, paints and plastics.
- Glass which is used in windows is manufactured in chemical process industries.
- Drugs and pharmaceutical products prepared from chemical process industries.
- Written communication uses paper and printing ink was manufactured from chemical process pulp and paper industries.
- Electronic communication requires many chemically processed insulators and conductors.
- Clothing utilizes many synthetic fibers and dyes.
- Transportation depends up on gasoline and other fuels which are refined by chemical process industries.
- Cleaning agents like soap, synthetic detergents and wetting agents are synthesized in chemical process industries, which are used in household and industrial cleaning.
- Fermentation products penicillin and ethyl alcohol is synthesized from Biochemical process industries.
- Nuclear fuel uranium is extracted from its ore in metal industry.
- Many chemicals never reach the consumer in their original form. But it is used in further production of

other chemicals for consumer use.

HISTORY OF CHEMICAL PROCESS INDUSTRIES

The history of chemical process industries was divided in to two periods.

- **Prescientific period**
- **Scientific period**

Prescientific period:

The early prescientific chemical industry was developed as trade or craft without literate or learned class, no chemical knowledge and no chemical analysis. Records of chemical process development were available from the beginning of 16th century.

The oldest chemical process industry is fermentation by folk craft method. Ceramics began from 5000 BC from baked clay bricks and pottery. Recovery of metals began from 4000 BC. First metal copper was extracted from its ore in Egypt about 3500 BC. Porcelain was developed in the 8th century in china.

Soap was made in 1st century. But the chemistry of soap making was unknown until the early 19th century. Nitric acid was made in 14th century. Hydrochloric acid was discovered in the 17th century.

Scientific period:

The progress growth of early chemical industry was slow, because of little understanding of scientific principles. In late 18th century scientific principles of chemistry rapidly increased and the chemical process was also increased.

Rubber was introduced in early 19th century. The organic chemical industry was began in 1850 AC. Dye work was established in 1857 AC. In 1862 AC first plastic was invented.

In 1880 AC synthetic drug industry was developed in Germany. Industrial production of soap from vegetable oils was started in 1885 AC.

Bakelite was introduced in 1908 BC. Cellophane cellulose film was introduced in 1923 BC. Nylon was invented in 1939

GREATEST PERSONALITIES OF CHEMICAL ENGINEERING

George Edward Davis: Known as the father of the discipline 'Chemical Engineering.' He defined and explained what Chemical Engineering is. He even wrote the book, 'A Handbook of Chemical Engineering, Volume I and II', which explained the basic industrial operations done on a much larger scale.

Arthur D. Little: is the foundation of unit operations. This was applied to all and basically helped in defined the basic industrial processes.

John. H Perry:*Perry's Chemical Engineer's Handbook* wouldn't have been possible without John. H Perry. It contains all the important properties and knowledge required by professors and Chemical Engineers.

Thomas H. Chilton: Known as the father of modern Chemical Engineering Practices, He developed a analogy which is widely known and used in courses like mass and heat transfer. He worked as a Chemical Engineer to understanding the chemical phenomena behind heat and momentum.

Warren.K. Lewis: American Chemical Engineering professor, also known as "Father of Modern Chemical Engineering". He defined the field of Chemical Engineering in its early development, and co-developed the *Houdry process* of petroleum refining.

Elmer L.Gaden, Jr: Elmer was the father of 'Biochemical Engineering', who served 25 years of his career in academics. His dissertation topic was based on penicillin production. It basically explained the processes and fundamentals behind the penicillin production.

Carl Bosch: He scale up the Haber process scaled up to the industrial level. This process enables the production of synthetic fertilizers and today contributes to half of the world's food production. He is a recipient of the Nobel Prize in Chemistry, 1931.

Margaret Hutchinson Rousseau: In 1937, Margaret became the first women to ever receive a doctorate in Chemical Engineering from MIT. She is mainly worked in commercial penicillin plant and also contributed to creating high-octane gasoline processes.

Man Mohan Sharma: Eminent Indian Chemical Engineer and 1st Indian to be selected as Fellow of Royal Society, UK- an honourable position awarded to an Indian for his dedicated work.

HISTORY OF CHEMICAL ENGINEERING

The chemical engineering profession evolved from the industrial applications of chemistry and science.

The first high-volume chemical process was implemented in 1823 in England for the production of soda ash, which was used for the production of glass and soap. During the same time, advances in organic chemistry led to the development of chemical processes for producing synthetic dyes from coal for textiles, starting in the 1850s.

In 1887 a series of lectures on chemical engineering which summarized industrial practice in the chemical industry was presented in Britain. These lectures stimulated interest in the United States and to some degree led to the formation of the first chemical engineering curriculum in 1888.

After 10 to 15 years U.S. universities started various chemical engineering courses. In 1908, "The American Institute of Chemical Engineers" was formed to promote and represent the interests of the chemical engineering community.

In 1901, a geologist and a mining engineer led a drilling operation (the drillers were later produced more oil than all of the other oil wells in the United States.

These early industrial chemists/chemical engineers had few analytical tools available to them and largely depended upon their physical intuition to perform their jobs as process engineers. Slide rules were used to perform calculations.

In 1930s and 1940s a number of nomographs were developed to assist them in the design and operation analysis of processes for the **CPI**. Nomographs are charts that provide a concise and convenient method to represent physical property data (e.g., boiling point temperatures or heat of vaporization) and can also be used to provide simplified solutions of complex equations (e.g., pressure drop for flow in a pipe).

The computing resources that became available in the 1960s. In 1970s **computer-aided design (CAD)** packages have allowed engineers to design complete processes by specifying only a minimum amount of information. All the repetitive calculations are done by the computer in an extremely short period of time, allowing the design engineer to focus on the task of developing the best possible process design.

During the period 1960 to1980, the **CPI** also made the industry based on innovation, developing large amount of new products. At that time new processing approaches, were developed in industries to produce less expensive products.

Globalization of the CPI markets began in the mid-1980s and led to increased competition. At the same time, CPI apply process automation (advanced process control, or APC, and optimization) provided improved product quality with little capital investment.

Because of economic advantages, APC became widely accepted by industry over the next 15 years and remains an important factor for most companies in the CPI.

Beginning in the mid-1990s, new areas came on the scene that took advantage of the fundamental skills of chemical engineers, including the microelectronics industry, the pharmaceutical industry, the biotechnology industry, and, more recently, nanotechnology.

Clearly, the analytical skills and the process training made chemical engineers to contribute the development of the production operations for these industries.

ROLE OF CHEMICAL ENGINEER

The work of the chemical engineer required an ever-growing background of education and experience. Today a Chemical Engineer may work in many fields with in the profession of Chemical Engineering.

Communication:

- The successful chemical engineer must be able to express his technical ideas in oral and written communication.
- Writing and speaking are more important in all fields of chemical engineering from research to sales.

Human Relations:

- Almost all activities of engineers require close work with other engineers, scientists and technicians.
- He must work effectively in a group. He must be able to sell his ideas effectively and tactfully.

Professional Activities:

- All engineers should be active in their professional societies.
- All the chemical engineers must attend and conduct local, national and international level public meetings and conferences for rectifying the superstition believes in the society.

Technical Reading:

- The chemical engineer should keep up to date in his field not only by attending professional meetings, but also by reading technical research journals.

Role of chemical engineer in Research:

- **Fundamental Chemical Research Engineer** must have an excellent background in physics, mathematics, chemistry, as well as the principles of chemical engineering.
- **Exploratory Chemical Research Engineer** would try many catalysts and various operating conditions to explore commercial possibilities.
- **Process Research Chemical Engineer** must obtain sufficient quantitative data from exploratory research to make possible a preliminary economic process evaluation.

Role of chemical engineer in Process Development:

- The development engineer must work closely with process-research group and design engineer.

- The development engineer must **plan the program** to obtain the maximum information in the least time at minimum cost.
- He understands and utilizes the results of process research. He must determine the critical process variables.

Role of chemical engineer in Process Design and Evaluation:

- The process design engineer is concerned with the design of the overall chemical process.
- He utilizes the data of process research and development and work closely with development engineer.
- He must estimate many quantities using his previous experience as a basis. He use digital computer for long routine calculations.
- He is well in fundamentals of chemical kinetics and unit operations. And he must exercise his imagination and judgment often.

Role of chemical engineer in Construction:

- The construction supervisor is responsible for completing the plant in the shortest time within the allotted budget.
- He must carefully schedule manpower requirements.

- He must maintain good labor relations to avoid poor work, slowdowns and work stoppage.

Role of chemical engineer in production supervisor:

- The product supervisor checks the daily records and tries to improve operation.
- He adjusts process variables and tries to give optimum conditions.
- He improves product quality by removing contaminations.

Role of chemical engineer in plant Technical Service:

- Service Engineer identifies and analyzes the problem, and suggests a solution to the operator.
- Technical service engineer is must in start-up a new process. He works closely with process development, process design and plant design.

Role of chemical engineer in plant Technical Service:

- **Market** Research **Engineer** begins its analysis as soon as promising result is reported by the exploratory-research engineer.
- **Product Development Engineer** suggests a change in the customer's process to make less expensive, smooth handle and satisfy the need for high purity.
- **Customer technical service Engineer** solves the problem and also answer customers question.

GREATEST ACHIEVEMENTS OF CHEMICAL ENGINEERING

Chemical engineering is an enormous field and it achieved in many different applications. Greatest achievements are follows.

The Atom:

Chemical engineers' produced Atomic bomb in World War II by DuPont's Handford Chemical Plant. Today these techniques are used in many peaceful applications like Biology, Medicine, Metallurgy and power generations.

The Plastic:

Polymer chemistry was developed in 19th century. Chemical engineers developed the plastic in 20th century with low expense. Now a day's all aspects of modern life is positively impacted by plastic. A plastic called Bakelite was developed in 1908 which is used in electrical insulations, plugs and sockets etc.,

The Human Reactor:

Chemical engineers studied the chemical processes by breaking them up into smaller "unit operations." Such operations might consist of heat exchangers, filters, chemical reactors etc. Fortunately this concept has also been applied to the human body. These improve the clinical care, improvements in diagnostic and therapeutic devices. This led to the invention of artificial organs.

The Drugs:

Chemical engineers (Sir Arthur Fleming who discovered penicillin in 1929) developed the antibiotics and increase their yields several thousand times through mutation and special brewing techniques. Today's low price and high volume drugs are produced by chemical engineers.

Synthetic Fibers:

Chemical engineers produced the synthetic fibre reduce the strain on natural resources of cotton and wool.

Synthetic fibres used in, nylon stocking makes our skin look young and attractive. Bullet proof vests are also produced from synthetic fibres by chemical engineers.

Liquefied Air:

When air is cooled to very low temperatures (about 320 deg F below zero) it condenses into a liquid. Chemical engineers can then separate out the different components. The purified nitrogen can be used to recover petroleum, freeze food, produce semiconductors, or prevent unwanted reactions while oxygen is used to make steel, smelt copper, weld metals together, and support the lives of patients in hospitals.

The Environment:

Chemical engineers provide economical answers to clean up yesterday's waste and prevent tomorrow's pollution. Catalytic converters, reformulated gasoline, and smoke stack scrubbers all help keep the world clean. Additionally, chemical engineers help reduce the strain on natural materials through synthetic replacements, more efficient processing, and new recycling technologies.

Food:

Plants need large amounts of nitrogen, potassium, and phosphorus to grow in abundance. Chemical fertilizers can help provide nutrients to crops, which in turn provide us with a plentiful and balanced diet. Fertilizers are especially important in certain regions of Asia and Africa where food can sometimes be scarce.Chemical engineers are at the forefront of food processing where they help create better tasting and most nutritious foods.

Petrochemicals:

Chemical engineers have helped to develop processes like catalytic cracking to break down the complex organic

molecules found in crude oil into much simpler species. These building blocks are then separated and recombined to form many useful products including gasoline, lubricating oils, plastics, synthetic rubber, and synthetic fibers. Petroleum processing is therefore recognized as an enabling technology.

II

CHEMICAL ENGINEERING CORRELATION WITH SCIENCE

ROLE OF CHEMICAL KINETICS IN CHEMICAL ENGINEERING

Chemical Engineer must know the rate at which the reactions take place. Many inorganic reactions are very fast and completed in a short time. Many organic reactions are very slow and it takes a long time to complete. So chemical engineers must study the kinetics of the chemical reaction in order to design the reactor properly.

Activated complex:

The existence of the intermediate compound between reactants and products is called activated complex.

Consider the following reversible reaction between A and B

A + B –> [AB] —> C + D

Where: A, B – Reactant Molecules

[A, B] – Activated Complex

[C, D] – Product Molecules

The double arrow shows that the reaction can go in either forward or backward direction.

The activated complex is formed by collisions between reactant molecules, and occurs at high enough energy levels. The activated complex is not stable and it decomposes in to reactant or products.

Order of the reaction:

The sum of the power of the exponential powers to which the concentration term is raised in the experimentally determined rate law of a chemical reaction.

In general reaction

aA + bB Products

$$rate = K[A]^p [B]^q$$

p = a or less than a

q = q or less than b

K= rate constant of the reaction.

p and q are the exponents or also known as the order of the reaction with respect to reactant A and B respectively.

First order Reaction:

First order reaction is one in which the rate of the reaction is proportional to the concentration of single reacting compounds.

Second Order Reaction:

First order reaction is one in which the rate of the reaction is proportional to the concentration any two reacting compounds.

Chemical Equilibrium:

Chemical equilibrium is dynamic in nature. At equilibrium, the reactant and product molecules are both present in the reaction mixture in definite amounts. The equilibrium concentrations of the reactants and products do not change under constant temperature, pressure and catalysts etc.

Le Chatelier's principles:

If a system at equilibrium is disturbed or stressed, then the equilibrium shifts in the direction that tends to nullify the effect of the disturbance or stress.

Factors that affect the equilibrium:

- Temperature, pressure and concentration factors are alter the state of equilibrium.
- The addition of a catalyst has no effect on the state of equilibrium.

PROCESS CONTROL

Process controls is a mixture between the statistics and engineering discipline that deals with the mechanism, architectures, and algorithms for controlling a process.

Some examples of controlled processes:

· Controlling the temperature of a water stream by controlling the amount of steam added to the shell of a heat exchanger.

· Operating a jacketed reactor isothermally by controlling the mixture of cold water and steam that flows through the jacket of a jacketed reactor.

· Maintaining a set ratio of reactants to be added to a reactor by controlling their flow rates.

· Controlling the height of fluid in a tank to ensure that it does not overflow.

Objectives of Process Control

1. To Maintain the process at the operational conditions and set points:

Many processes should work at steady state conditions or in a state in which it satisfies all the benefits for a company such as budget, yield, safety, and other quality objectives..

2. To Transition the process from one operational condition to another:

In real-life situations, engineers may change the process operational conditions for a variety of different reasons such as economics, Product specifications, Operational constraints Environmental regulations, Consumer/ Customer specifications, Environmental regulations and Safety precautions

PROCESS CONTROL METHODS

1.Understand the process: Before attempting to control a process it is necessary to understand how the process works and what it does.

2. Identify the operating parameters: Once the process is well understood, operating parameters such as temperatures, pressures, flow rates, and other variables specific to the process must be identified for its control.

3. Identify the hazardous conditions: In order to maintain a safe and hazard-free facility, variables that may cause safety concerns must be identified and may require additional control.

4.Identify the measurables: It is important to identify the measurables that correspond with the operating parameters in order to control the process. Measurables for process systems include: Temperature, Pressure, Flow rate, pH, Humidity, Level, Concentration, Viscosity, Conductivity, Turbidity, Redox potential, Electrical behavior and Flammability.

5.Identify the points of measurement: Once the measurables are identified, it is important locate where they will be measured so that the system can be accurately controlled.

6.Select measurement methods: Selecting the proper type of measurement device specific to the process will ensure that the most accurate, stable, and cost-effective method is chosen. There are several different signal types that can detect different things. These signal types include: Electric, Pneumatic, Light, Radio waves, Infrared (IR) and Nuclear Magnetic Resonance.

7.Select control method: In order to control the operating parameters, the proper control method is vital to control the process effectively. On/off is one control method and the other is continuous control. Continuous control involves Proportional (P), Integral (I), and Derivative (D) methods or some combination of those three.

8. Select control system: Choosing between a local or distributed control systems that fits well with the process affects both the cost and efficacy of the overall control.

9. Set control limits: Understanding the operating parameters allows the ability to define the limits of the measurable parameters in the control system.

10. Define control logic: Choosing between feed-forward, feed-backward, cascade, ratio, or other control logic is a necessary decision based on the specific design and safety parameters of the system.

11. Create a s system: Even the best control system will have failure points; therefore it is important to design a redundancy system to avoid catastrophic failures by having back-up controls in place.

12. Define a fail-safe: Fail-safes allow a system to return to a safe state after a breakdown of the control. This fail-safe allows the process to avoid hazardous conditions that may otherwise occur.

13. Set lead/lag criteria: Depending on the control logic used in the process, there may be lag times associated with the measurement of the operating parameters. Setting lead/ lag times compensates for this effect and allow for accurate control.

14. Investigate effects of changes before/after: By investigating changes made by implementing the control system, unforeseen problems can be identified and corrected before they create hazardous conditions in the facility.

15. Integrate and test with other systems: The proper integration of a new control system with existing process systems avoids conflicts between multiple systems.

TRANSPORT PHENOMENA - HEAT TRANSFER

Transfer of thermal energy from one place to another due to thermal difference is called Heat Transfer. It occurs in combination with other unit operations such as distillation, drying, crystallization and evaporation. It may happen by any one or more of the three basic mechanism of heat transfer.

Mechanism of Heat Transfer:

It occurs by three mechanisms: conduction, convection and radiation.

Conduction:

If the temperature gradient exist in a continuous medium heat is transferred between adjacent molecules is called conduction. Conduction occurs on the molecular scale. More Hotter molecules have greater energy and less hot molecules have lower energy. In conduction, hotter molecule transferring energy to the adjacent molecule at lowers energy level.

Example:

1. The flow of heat through the brick wall of a furnace.
2. The metal wall of a heat exchanger tube takes place by conduction.

Convection:

The heat energy exchange between solid surfaces to a fluid is called convection. Transport of thermal energy by bulk transport and mixing of warmer portions with cooler portions of a fluid is called convection. If the heat transfer is occurs by the fluid is forced to flow on a solid surface by fan, pump or other mechanical methods is called forced convection heat transfer. If the heat transfer is occurs by the difference in densities of the warmer and cooler fluid elements

in contact with a solid surface is called natural convection or free convection.

Example:

1. Heating of room by steam radiator.
2. Heating of water in cooking pan,

Radiation:

Transport of energy through the space by electromagnetic waves is called radiation. Radiation passing through empty space is not transformed to heat or any other form of energy and not it is diverted it path. If the radiation passes through matter, the radiation is transmitted, reflected or absorbed. The absorbed energy appears as heat. This transformation is quantitative.

Example:

1. Transfer of heat from the sun to the earth.
2. Black body radiation.

In industrial equipments, all the three mechanisms of conduction, Convection and radiations are involved.

In insulated steam pipe, heat flows

- By convection through the steam film on the inside of the pipe.
- By conduction through the layer of the scale deposited on the inside of the pipe.
- By conduction through the metal wall of the pipe.
- By conduction through layer of the insulating material.
- And finally by convection and radiation from the outside insulation surface of the pipe to the ambient air.

TRANSPORT PHENOMENA - MASS TRANSFER

When a concentration gradient exists in a fluid containing two or more components, each component tends to migrate to reduce the concentration gradients.

This process is known as mass transfer. Mass transfer operations depended by molecules diffusion, vaporization, vapour pressure and solubility. This operation includes techniques like,

Absorption:

Absorption refers to an operation in which the transfer of materials from a gaseous phase to liquid phase. In absorption, a vapour solute in a gas mixture is absorbed by a liquid.

Example: Absorption of ammonia from Air-Ammonia mixture by water.

If the solute is transferred from solvent to the gaseous phase, then this operation is called desorption.

Adsorption:

Adsorption involves the transfer of mass from either a gas or a liquid to the surface of a solid.

Adsorption operation classified in to,

1. Separation of gases from gases:
2. Separation of vapours from gases:
3. Separation of solutes and colloids from solutions.

Extraction:

The process of transferring from one or more components of a liquid or a solid phase to another liquid phase is called Extraction. It utilizes the differences in the solubilities of the compounds. In solvent extraction a solute in a solution is removed by adding immiscible liquid. The liquid which is added to the solution to bring out the extract is called solvent.

Example: separation of aromatics from kerosene-based fuels oils.

Extraction of medicinal compounds from plant roots leaves and stems in pharmaceutical industry.

Distillation:

The separation of liquid volatile substance, from a mixture of two or more liquid or solid substances by difference in vapour pressure is called Distillation.

Example: Separation of mixture of ethanol and water in to its component.

Separation of Crude oil into gasoline, kerosene, fuel oil and lubrication stocks.

Extraction of sugar from sugar beets with hot water.

Humidification:

In humidification a gas stream can be increased by passing a gas over the liquid which then evaporates into the gas stream.

Example: In air water system, water is transferred from liquid phase to gaseous phase in a mixture of air and water vapour.

In dehumidification the vapour content in a gas stream can be reduced by condensation on a cold surface. It involves the transfer of water vapour from the gas phase to the liquid phase.

Drying:

Drying means the removal of relatively small amounts of water or other liquid from a solid or nearly solid material. It refers to the removal of relatively large amount of water from solutions. In evaporation the water is removed as vapour at its boiling point. But drying means the removal of water at temperature below the boiling point by circulating air or some other carrier gas over the material.

Crystallization:

Crystallization is a process whereby solid particles are formed from a liquid solution. The solution is concentrated and usually cooled until the solute concentration becomes higher than its solubility at that temperature. A crystal formed from impure solution is itself pure unless mixed crystals occur.

Membrane separation:

This process involves the diffusion of a solute from a liquid or gas through a semi-permeable membrane to another fluid.

Example: Osmosis, reverse osmosis, etc.,

Foam separation:

This process is carried out in surface surface-active compounds in a solution can be selectively concentrated and separated by accumulation at the interface between the liquid and gas. The foam separation process is basically an adoptive bubble separation method.

Example: Removal or recovery of minerals, surfactants, enzymes, micro-organisms, proteins, organic compounds and various metallic ions.

ROLE OF THERMODYNAMICS IN CHEMICAL ENGINEERING

- Thermodynamics means flow of heat. It deals with the relationship between heat and work.
- It is a science which deals with various forms of energy conversion.
- The concept of thermodynamics is, heat of a process and work, both of which is the form of energy transfer.

TERMINOLOGIES USE IN THERMODYNAMICS

System: It is a part of matter under investigation which is separated from other part of the system by real or imaginary boundaries.

Types of System

Open System: If the system exchange both energy and matter with its surroundings is called open system.

Closed System: If the system exchange energy but not matter with its surroundings is called closed system.

Isolated System: If the system does not exchange both energy and matter with its surroundings is called open system.

Surroundings: Everything in the universe that is not the part of the system and can interact with it is called as surroundings.

Boundary: Anything which separates the system from its surroundings is called boundary.

Intensive properties: are those that are not dependent the size (mass) of a system, such as temperature, pressure, and density.

Extensive properties: The values that are dependent on size of the system such as mass, volume, and total energy. They are additive.

LAWS OF THERMODYNAMICS

First law of Thermodynamics: Energy can be converted from one form to another. But it cannot be created.

$$mM + nN \rightarrow xX + zZ$$

$$\Delta H_R = \Delta H_{reaction} = \sum \Delta H_{products} - \sum \Delta H_{reactants}$$

If ΔH_R is negative (-) it is exothermic reaction (system liberates heat)

If ΔH_R is positive (+) it is endothermic reaction (system absorbs heat)

Second law of Thermodynamics: It is impossible to construct a machine which converts the energy completely in to work without energy or heat loss.

Zeroth La;w of Thermodynamics: If two systems at different temperatures are separately in thermal equilibrium with a third one then they tends to be in thermal equilibrium with them.

THERMODYNAMICS FUNCTIONS

Internal Energy (U): The energy in the system arising from the relative positions and interactions of its parts is called internal energy.

Enthalpy (H) : Enthalpy is defined as sum of the internal energy U and the product of Pressure and Volume of the system. It is also said to be Heat content of the system.

$$H = U + PV$$

Entropy (S): Entropy is defined as the degree of disorder.

Gibbs Free Energy (G) : Free energy is defined as the difference in the heat content of the system with the Temperature and the Entropy of the system.

$$G = H - TS$$

THERMODYNAMIC PROCESSES

Adiabatic process: Occurs without loss or gain of energy by heat.

Isenthalpic process: Occurs at a constant enthalpy

Isentropic process: A reversible adiabatic process occurs at constant entropy.

Isobaric process: Occurs at constant pressure.

Isochoric process: Occurs at constant volume. It also called as isometric or isovolumetric process

Isothermal process: Occurs at a constant temperature

Steady state process: Occurs without a change in the internal energy.

ROLE OF BIOLOGY IN CHEMICAL ENGINEERING

Biochemical engineering supplements the traditional Chemical Engineering skills with additional study of biology, microbiology, and biochemistry. This knowledge enables the extension of chemical engineering principles to applications in biotechnology including commercial enzymes, food and food additives, pharmaceuticals, and bio-fuels, pesticides, insecticides and fertilizers.

In modern chemical Engineering, chemical process industries includes microbiological synthesis, genetic engineering, fermentation technology tissue culturing, cell hybridization etc., which is inclined with the help of Biologist and biological principles.

Fermentation:

- Fermentation is a metabolic process that produces chemical changes in organic substrates through the action of enzymes. Enzymes are introduces naturally from bacteria or from artificial enzymes.
- In biochemistry, Fermentation is narrowly defined as the extraction of energy from carbohydrates in the absence of oxygen.

- In the context of food production, it may more broadly refer to any process in which the activity of microorganisms brings about a desirable change to a foodstuff or beverage.

Pesticide:

- Any substance or mixture of substances intended for preventing, destroying, or controlling any pest is called pesticides.
- Pest includes
  - Vectors of human or animal disease,
  - Unwanted species of plants or animals.
  - Causing harm, with the production, processing, storage, transport, or marketing of food, Substances.

Insecticides:

- Insecticides are substances used to kill insects.
- They include ovicides and larvicides used against insect eggs and larvae, respectively.
- Insecticides are used in agriculture, medicine, industry and by consumers.

Fertilizer:

- A Fertilizer is any material of natural or synthetic origin that is applied to soils or to plant tissues to supply one or more plant nutrients essential to the growth of plants.
- Many sources of fertilizer exist, both natural and industrially produced.

- Industrially produced fertilizers prepared from chemical engineering principles.

Bioreactor:

- A bioreactor is a engineered device or system that supports a biologically active environment.
- A bioreactor is a vessel in which a chemical process is carried out.
- It involves organisms or biochemically active substance derived from such organisms.
- This process can either be aerobic or anaerobic.

Artificial organs:

Artificial organs are an engineered device or tissue that is implanted or integrated into a human. Ear, Eye, Heart, Liver, Lungs, Ovaries and Pancreas are some of the artificial organs made by chemical and biological engineers.

Vitamins:

Synthetic vitamins do not come from food, as it's difficult to extract vitamins from natural resources. A synthetic vitamin is usually an isolated molecule, and is not exactly like the naturally-occurring molecule found in a whole food.

Enzymes:

Artificial enzymes based on amino acids or peptides as characteristic molecular moieties have expanded the field of artificial enzymes or enzyme mimics.

Hormones:

Synthetic chemical compounds which mimic the activity of endogenous hormones produced in the body, but which differ in structure from naturally occurring hormones.

Dairy products

Dairy or milk products are a type of food produced from or containing the milk of mammals, primarily cattle, water buffaloes, goats, sheep, camels, and humans. Eggs, however, are not dairy.

ROLE OF CHEMISTRY IN CHEMICAL ENGINEERING

All the Phases of Chemistry are usually involved in Chemical engineering. Chemical equations are particularly important to establish conversion and yield data.

1. Analytical Chemistry:

- Analytical chemistry is necessary for process control, yield determination and optimization.
- Manual, Modern and electronic instrumentations are used to Analyze the Chemical process.
- Example: Vapor Phase Chromatography, Infrared Spectroscopy, NMR spectroscopy are used.

1. Physical Chemistry:

- Physical chemistry is integrated with chemical engineering unit operations.
- In separation process Phase Diagram studies are used.
- It involves in the use of Chemical kinetics and catalysis.

3. Inorganic Chemistry:

- Inorganic Chemistry deals the reaction which does not contain combinations of C, H and O with or without other non metallic compounds.

- Principles of Theoretical inorganic chemistry are used in Chemical engineering process.
- Types of bonding, metal-organic complexes, reaction chemistry predictions are known by Inorganic Chemistry.

4. Organic Chemistry.

- Organic Chemistry deals the reactions which contain combinations of C, H and O with or without other non metallic compounds.

- Many commercial organic chemicals derived from aliphatic and aromatic compounds of petroleum.

5. Nano Chemistry:

- This chemistry control, and predict the particle size of the prepared compounds.
- The activity or application of the compounds was increased with decrease in the size of the prepared compounds.

6. Electro Chemistry:

- It is also a branch of chemistry, deals with the chemical applications of electricity.
- It mainly deals with the chemical reactions produced by passing electric current through an electrolyte or the production of electric current through chemical reactions.

ROLE OF PROCESS DESIGN IN CHEMICAL ENGINEERING

Process Design is concerned with unit operations and processes. It is also concerned with the design of the overall chemical process.

A series of Flow sheets which incorporate unit operations and unit processes to achieve the desired production.

Types of flow sheets:

1. Block diagrams: These are simple rectangular diagram which gives a graphic layout of the various steps in a process.
2. Simplified Engineering flow sheets: It shows the process in detail by which physical equipment operates the operations of chemical process.
3. Other design Flow Sheets: This includes flow sheets of piping layout, electrical layout, instrumentation details, plan layout, etc.

PROCESS STEPS

As an elementary approach to most chemical processes, the following broad steps can be considered.

- Prepare the Reactants
- React them
- Separate the products
- Purify the products

DESIGN STEPS

- Collect all laboratory and process development information.

- Prepare flow sheets
- Choose conventional design procedures for equipment designated on flow sheets as Unit Operations oriented.
- Design the reactors: This is one of the major impacts of the plant design. Optimum design is critical.
- Select control instrumentation for process monitoring and analysis.
- Materials handling equipment: Pumps, Piping, Conveyors, etc.
- Design all process auxiliaries.
- Make plant layouts
- Itemize all designs for cost estimating.

<u>A process design includes the following major items.</u>

- Process Flow sheets
- Mass balances on the overall process.
- Energy balances of the overall process.
- Specifications of the capacities, flow, and pressure.
- Specifications of size and configurations of chemical reactors and storage tanks.
- Determination of optimum operating conditions.
- Estimation of utility requirements.
- Economic evaluation with an estimate of capital investment and operating costs.

III

MANUFACTURING OF SULPHURIC ACID AND SODA ASH

FLOWSHEET REPRESENTATION OF CHEMICAL PROCESS

Introduction:

Explanation of a complete chemical process covers several hundred of pages. To understand the complete design of chemical process simplified flow sheets are prepared to illustrate the process.

A common type of Flow Sheets shows the major unit operations and chemical reactors with their interconnecting piping and an identification of the materials being processed.

A series of Flow sheets which incorporate unit operations and unit processes to achieve the desired production.

Types of flow sheets:

1. Block diagrams: These are simple rectangular diagram which gives a graphic layout of the various steps in a process.
2. Simplified Engineering flow sheets: It shows the process in detail by which physical equipment operates the operations of chemical process.
3. Other design Flow Sheets: This includes flow sheets of piping layout, electrical layout, instrumentation details, plan layout, etc.

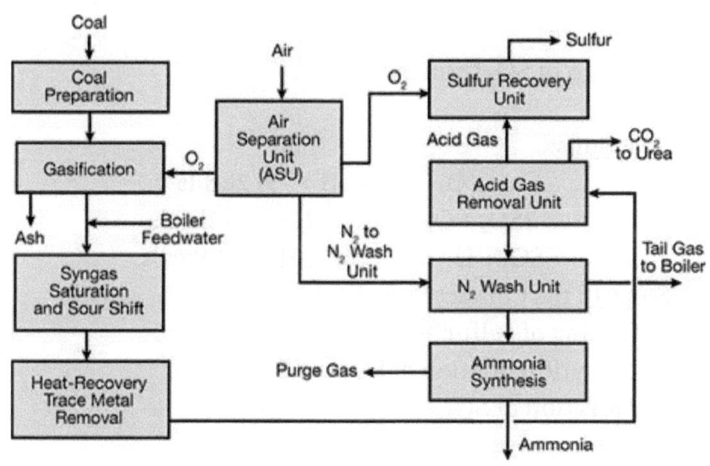

Flow sheets representation of Manufacturing of Ammonia

MANUFACTURING OF SULFURIC ACID BY CONTACT PROCESS

Almost all sulfuric acid is manufactured by the contact process.

Raw Materials Basis:

1000kg sulfuric acid (100%)

Sulfur dioxide or pyrite (FeS2) = 670kg

Air = 1450-2200Nm3

Sources of raw material

Sulfur from mines:

Sulfur or hydrogen sulfide recovered from petroleum

Desulfurization:

- Recovery of sulfur dioxide from coal or oil-burning public utility stack gases.
- Recovery of sulfur dioxide from the smelting of metal sulfide ores.
- Isolation of SO_2 from pyrite.

Reactions:

$$S + O_2 \rightarrow SO_2 \ \Delta H = -71.2kcals$$

$$2SO_2 + O_2 \rightarrow 2SO_3 \ \Delta H = -46.3kcals$$

$$SO_3 + H_2O \rightarrow H_2SO_4 \ \Delta H = -31.1kcals$$

Steps in the Contact Process

1. Burning of sulfur
2. Catalytic oxidation of SO_2 to SO_3
3. Hydration of SO_3

1. Burning of sulfur:

Burning of sulfur in presence of dry air is carried out in sulfur pyrite burner. As SO_2 is needed for the catalytic oxidation and prevention of corrosion, dry air is used in the combustion process. If sulfur contains carbonaceous impurities, the molten material has to be filtered to avoid poisoning the catalyst and forming water from burning hydrogen.

2. Catalytic oxidation of SO_2 to SO_3

When using sulfur from sources 1 and 2, purification of the SO2 gas is normally not needed. Other sources of SO_2 require wet scrubbing followed by treatment of the gas with electrostatic precipitators to remove fine particles. The catalyst used is vanadium pentoxide (V_2O_5) and the pressure is 1.2-1.5 atmospheres. The temperature has to be kept around 450°C. If it rises above 450°C, the equilibrium is displaced away from SO_3. Temperature should reach around 450°C for the catalyst to be activated. This process is strongly exothermic. The catalytic reactor is designed as a four-stage fixed-bed unit. The gas has to be cooled between each steps. The temperature rises to over 600°C with the passage of the gas through each catalyst bed. The doubled absorption consists of cooling the gases between each bed back to the desired range by sending them through the heat exchanger and then back through the succeeding beds. Between the third and fourth beds, the gases are cooled and send to an absorption tower. This is to shift the equilibrium to the right by absorbing SO_3. The gases are then sent to the heat exchanger to warm them to 410-430°C and then on to the fourth catalyst bed.

3. Hydration of SO_3:

After the catalytic oxidation process, the resulting SO_3 is hydrated by absorption in packed towers filled with 98-99% sulfuric acid. At lower acid concentrations, sulfuric acid and SO_3 form a troublesome mist and at higher concentrations emissions of SO_3 and H_2SO_4 vapour become significant. The absorption acid concentration is kept within the desired range by the exchange as needed between the H_2SO_4 in the drying acid vessel that precedes the combustion chamber with the H_2SO_4 in the absorption tower. The acid strength can be adjusted by controlling the streams of H_2SO_4 to give acid of 91 to 100% H_2SO_4 with various amounts of added SO_3 and water. The conversion of sulfur to acid is over 99.5%.

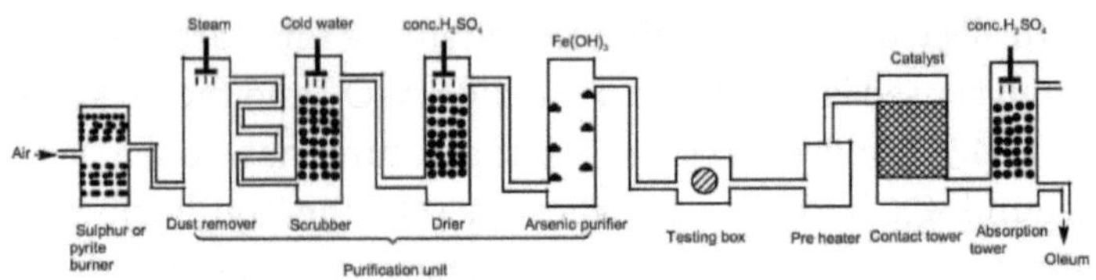

Manufacturing of Sulphuric acid

MANUFACTURING OF SODA ASH BY CONTACT PROCESS

INTRODUCTION:

Sodium carbonate (Na_2CO_3) also known as washing soda or soda ash, is a sodium salt of carbonic acid. Most commonly occurs as a crystalline hepta hydrate, which readily effloresces to form a white powder, the monohydrate. Sodium carbonate is domestically well known as a water softener. It can be extracted from the ashes of many plants. It is synthetically produced in large quantities from salt and limestone in a process known as the Solvay process.

Soda ash is the most important high tonnage, low cost, reasonably pure, soluble alkali available to the industries as well to the laboratory.

RAW MATERIALS

Basis: 1000kg sodium carbonate

Salt = 1550kg

Limestone = 1200kgCoke = 90kg

Ammonia as a catalyst = 1.5kg (Loss)

High pressure steam = 1350kg

Low pressure steam = 1600kg

Cooling water = 40000 - 60000kg

Electric power = 210KWH

SOURCES OF RAW MATERIAL

Common salt can be obtained from sea water, salt lake and sub–soil water. Lime stone is obtained from mineral calcite or aragonite, which can be used after removal of clay, slit and sand.

FLOW SHEET REPRESENTATION

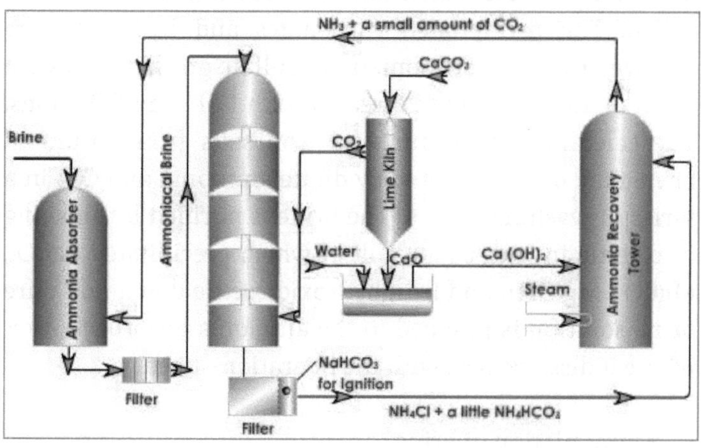

Manufacturing od Soda Ash

REACTIONS

$$CaCO_3 \rightarrow CaO + CO_2 \ \Delta H = +43.4kcals$$

$$C(s) + O_2 (g) \rightarrow CO_2 (g) \ \Delta H = -96.5kcals$$

$$CaO(s) + H_2O (l) \rightarrow Ca(OH)_2 (aq) \ \Delta H = -15.9kcals$$

$$NH_3(aq) + H_2O(l) \rightarrow NH_4OH(aq) \ \Delta H = -8.4kcals$$

$$2NH_4OH + CO_2 \rightarrow (NH4)_2CO_3 + H_2O \ \Delta H = -22.1kcals$$

$$(NH_4)_2CO_3 + CO_2 + H_2O \rightarrow 2NH_4HCO_3$$

$$NH_4HCO_3 + NaCl \rightarrow NH_4Cl + NaHCO_3$$

$$2NaHCO_3 \rightarrow Na_2CO_3 + CO_2 + H_2O \ \Delta H = +30.7kcals$$

$$2NH_4Cl + Ca(OH)_2 \rightarrow 2NH_3 + CaCl_2 + 2H_2 \ \Delta H = +10.7kcals$$

MANUFACTURING STEPS

1. Preparation and purification of brine

Saturated solution of NaCl is used. Brine contains impurities such as calcium, magnesium and iron compounds. To remove calcium sulfate, magnesium and iron salts sodium carbonate and sodium hydroxide are added. The precipitated carbonates and hydroxide are removed by filtration. Sometimes sulfate are removed with $BaCl_2$ or the hot brine is treated with OH^- and CO_3^{-2} ions. The calcium, magnesium and iron salts from saturated brine may be precipitated by dilute ammonia and CO_2 in a series of washing towers. The brine is purified by allowing it to settle in vats, as a result of which precipitated $CaCO_3$, $MgCO_3$, $Mg(OH)_2$ and iron hydroxide settle down and pure brine solution is pumped to the ammonia absorber tower, where it dissolve NH_3 with the liberation of heat

1. Ammoniation of brine

The purified brine is allowed to percolate down the ammonia tower in which ammonia gas is passed through the bottom in a counter current fashion. The brine solution thus takes up the necessary amount of ammonia and liberates heat. The gas which escapes solution in the tank is absorbed by the brine falling down the tower. Some carbon dioxide is also absorbed by ammonia, as a result of which some insoluble carbonate is also precipitated. The ammoniated brine is allowed to settle, coded to about 30°C and pumped to the carbonating tower.

3. Carbon dioxide formation

Limestone is calcined to get CO_2 in a lime kiln filled with coke. As a result of burning of coke necessary heat required for the decomposition of lime stone is generated. CaO obtained from the lime kiln is converted into slaked lime and pumped to the ammonia recovery tower.

4. Carbonation of ammonium brine

CO_2 from the lime kiln is compressed and passed through the bottom of carbonating tower down which ammoniated brine percolates. Carbonating towers operated in series with several precipitation towers are constructed of cast iron having 22-25meter height, 1.6-2.5meter in diameter. During the precipitation cycle, the temperature is maintained about 20-25°C at the both ends and 45-55°C at the middle by making use of cooling coils, provided at about 20ft above the bottom. The tower gradually becomes flooded as sodium bicarbonate cakes on the cooling coils and shelves. The cooling coils of the foulded tower are shut off. Then the fresh hot ammoniated brine is fed down the tower in which $NaHCO_3$ are dissolved to form ammonium carbonate solution. The solution containing (NH4)2CO3, unconverted $NaHCO_3$ is allowed to fall down a second tower, called making tower. The making, towers are constructed with a series of boxes and sloped baffles. Ammoniated brine and CO_2 gas (90-95%) from the bicarbonate calciner is recompressed and pumped to the bottom of the making tower. The ammonium carbonate first reacts with CO_2 to form ammonium bicarbonate and the latter reacting with salt, forms sodium bicarbonate. The heat of exothermic reaction is removed by cooling coils.

5. Filtration:

$NaHCO_3$ slurry is then filtered on a rotary vacuum filter which helps in drying of bicarbonate and in recovering ammonia. The filter cake after removal of salt and NH_4Cl by washing with water, sent to a centrifugal filter to remove the moisture or calcined directly. During washing, about 10% $NaHCO_3$ also passes into filtrate. The filtrate containing NaCl, NH_4Cl, NaHCO3 and NH_4HCO_3 is treated with lime obtained from lime kiln to recover NH_3 and CO_2.

6. Calcination

NaHCO3 from the drum filter is calcined at about 200°C in a horizontal calciner, which is either fired at feed end by gas or steam heated unit. The heating being through the shell parallel to the product, which prevent the formation of bicarbonate lumps.

The hot soda ash form the calciner is passed through a rotary cooler and packed in bags. The exit gases (CO_2, NH_3, steam etc.) are cooled and condensed to get liquid ammonia; the rich CO_2 gas is cooled and returned to the carbonating tower. The product from the calciner is light soda ash. To produce dense soda ash, sufficient water is milled with it to form more mono hydrate $Na_2CO_3.H_2O$ and the mixture is recycled.

EVALUATION OF INDUSTRY

There are three commonly used and important methods of performing industry analysis. The three methods are:

A. Competitive Forces Model (Porter's 5 Forces)

1. Intensity of industry rivalry:

The number of participants in the industry and their respective market shares are a direct representation of the competitiveness of the industry. These are directly affected by all the factors mentioned above. Lack of differentiation in products tends to add to the intensity of competition. High exit costs like high fixed assets, government restrictions, labor unions, etc. also make the competitors fight the battle a little harder.

2. Threat of potential entrants:

This indicates the ease with which new firms can enter the market of a particular industry. If it is easy to enter an industry, companies face the constant risk of new competitors. If the entry is difficult, whichever company enjoys little competitive advantage reaps the benefits for a longer period. Also, under difficult entry circumstances, companies face a constant set of competitors.

3. Bargaining power of suppliers

This refers to the bargaining power of suppliers. If the industry relies on a small number of suppliers, they enjoy a considerable amount of bargaining power. This can affect small businesses because it directly influences the quality and the price of the final product.

4.Bargaining power of buyers:

The complete opposite happens when the bargaining power lies with the customers. If consumers/buyers enjoy market power, they are in a position to negotiate lower prices, better quality or additional services and discounts. This is the case in an industry with more competitors but a single buyer constituting a large share of the industry's sales.

5. Threat of substitute goods/services:

The industry is always competing with another industry in producing a similar substitute product. Hence, all firms in an industry have potential competitors from other industries. This takes a toll on their profitability because they are unable to charge exorbitant prices. Substitutes can take two forms – products with the same function/quality but lesser price or products of the same price but of better quality or providing more utility.

B. Broad Factors Analysis (PEST Analysis)

Broad Factors Analysis, also commonly called the PEST Analysis stands for Political, Economic, Social and Technological. PEST analysis is a useful framework for analyzing the external environment.

1. Political

Political factors that impact an industry include specific policies and regulations related to things like taxes, environmental regulation, tariffs, trade policies, labor laws, ease of doing business, and the overall political stability.

2. Economic

The economic forces that have an impact include inflation, exchange rates (FX), interest rates, GDP growth rates, conditions in the capital markets (ability to access capital) etc.

3. Social

The social impact on an industry refers to trends among people and includes things such as population growth, demographics (age, gender, etc), and trends in behavior such as health, fashion, and social movements.

4. Technological

The technological aspect of PEST analysis incorporates factors such as advancements and developments that change that way business operates and the ways which people live their lives (i.e. advent of the internet).

C. SWOT Analysis:

SWOT Analysis stands for Strengths, Weaknesses, Opportunities, and Threats. It can be a great way of summarizing various industry analysis methods and determining their implications for the business in question.

Strengths:

Characteristics of Industry business which give it advantages over its competitors.

Weaknesses:

Characteristics of Industry business which give it disadvantages over its competitors

Opportunities:

Elements in company's external environment that allow to formulate and implement strategies to increase profitability.

Threats:

Elements in company's external environment that couldendanger the integrity and profitability of the business.

IV

ROLE OF CHEMICAL ENGINEERING IN VARIOUS FIELD

RELATIONSHIP BETWEEN CHEMICAL AND OTHER ENGINEERING DISIPLINE

Mechanical engineering is a discipline of engineering that applies the principles of physics and materials science for analysis, design, manufacturing, and maintenance of mechanical systems.

It is the branch of engineering that involves the production and usage of heat and mechanical power for the design, production, and operation of machines and tools.

It is one of the oldest and broadest engineering disciplines.The engineering field requires an understanding of core concepts including mechanics, kinematics, thermodynamics, materials science, and structural analysis.

Mechanical engineers use these core principles along with tools like computer-aided engineering and product lifecycle management to design and analyze manufacturing plants, industrial equipment and machinery, heating and cooling systems, transport systems, aircraft, watercraft, robotics, medical devices and more.

Mechanical Engineering science emerged in the 19th century as a result of developments in the field of physics. The field has continually evolved to incorporate advancements in technology.

Mechanical engineers today are pursuing developments in fields such as composites, mechatronics and nano technology.

Mechanical Engineering overlaps with aerospace engineering, civil engineering, electrical engineering, petroleum engineering and chemical engineering to varying amounts.

ROLE OF CHEMICAL ENGINEER IN BIO-CHEMICALS

- The chemical which is used in biological system is called as Bio-Chemical. In other hand, the chemical which is extracted or isolated from biological systems is also called Bio-Chemicals.
- Biomedical researchers collaborated with Chemical Engineers are synthesis new bio-chemicals to manage and treat disease.

Pesticide as Biochemicals:

- Any substance or mixture of substances used for preventing, destroying, or controlling any pest is called pesticides.

Insecticides as Biochemicals:

- Any substance or mixture of substances used for preventing, destroying, or controlling any pest is called insecticides.

Fertilizer as Biochemicals:

- A Fertilizer is a bio-chemical which is used to increase the nutrient content of the soil.
- And also it is directly applied to plant tissues to supply one or more plant nutrients essential to the growth of plants.

Vitamins:

- Now a day's Vitamins a biochemical which is synthesised by chemical engineers.
- A synthetic vitamin is usually an isolated molecule, and is not exactly like the naturally-occurring molecule found in a whole food.
- Synthetic vitamins do not come from food, as it's difficult to extract vitamins from natural resources. Chemical Engineers now inclined to prepare vitamins from natural resources.

Enzymes:

- Artificial enzymes based on amino acids or peptides as characteristic molecular moieties have expanded the field of artificial enzymes or enzyme mimics.

Hormones:

- Hormones are used to communicate between organs and tissue for physiological activities like metabolism, respiration, reproduction etc.,
- Synthetic chemical compounds prepared by chemical engineers which mimic the activity of endogenous hormones produced in the body, but which differ in structure from naturally occurring hormones.

Drugs:

- Drug is a chemical substance or biological substances which are used to treat cure prevent or diagnose a disease.
- Chemical Engineers work hard to synthesis effective drugs without side effects in cheep.

ROLE OF CHEMICAL ENGINEER IN ENERGY

Chemical engineers are the forefront of innovation in the generation of energy. They generated renewable as well as nonrenewable Energy devices. A vast array of chemical-engineering principles is used to generate electricity and to produce different types of fuel for transportation, industrial, and residential purposes.

Traditional Refining:

- Crude oil, or petroleum, is of little use in its raw state.
- In Traditional periods, Refineries turn crude oil into gasoline, diesel, , kerosene, lubricating oils, and numerous other end products without understanding their chemical principles.

Modern Refining:

- The imaginative efforts of chemical engineers have been responsible for the development of a complex array of chemical conversion processes.
- These processes are used to create physical changes in crude oil and natural gas, which yield the many end products such as gasoline, diesel, kerosene, lubricating oils, waxes, and many intermediate petrochemical products.
- Some of the important chemical process operations in modern-day refining include Thermal cracking, Distillation, Fluid catalytic cracking, Hydro cracking etc.

<u>Refining the refineries:</u>

The chemical-engineering community is constantly working to modify and improve the petroleum-refining processes. Their objectives are to

- Achieve higher conversion rates and greater yields,
- Improve overall energy efficiency,
- Produce cleaner fuels,
- Reduce refinery emissions, and
- Reduce operating costs.

<u>Synthetic Liquid Fuels:</u>

In order to reduce our dependence on foreign oil, chemical engineers have been working vigorously to develop, scale up, and commercialize new processes to produce synthetic liquid fuels.

Essentially two routes are used to produce synthetic liquid fuels:

1. The Bergius process, which uses hydrogen and brown or soft coal, and

2. The Fischer-Tropsch process, which starts with carbon monoxide and hydrogen.

Chemical engineers advancing both of these technologies.

Bio-Fuels:

Chemical engineers are involved with developing technologies to convert renewable biomaterials into electricity.

Corn and sugar are now widely used to produce ethanol, a gasoline substitute. And soybeans are being used to produce diesel fuel.

Power from Plants

Biomass is plant material—fast-growing trees and grasses, grains, corn, sugar cane, wood scrap, even woody leaves and stalks and garbage.

It is a sun-dependent renewable feedstock that can be used to produce Bio-Fuel. This type of fuel can be converted into gaseous and liquid fuels for Electric power generation.

Ethanol:

- Ethanol is a gasoline-like alcohol.
- It is made by fermenting carbohydrates (starches and sugars).
- It is widely used in the production of a Gasoline-Ethanol mixture.
- With engine modifications it can be used as a direct gasoline substitute.

Bio-Diesel:

- Bio-Diesel is made from vegetable oils and animal fat.

- Biodiesel is a functional alternative to conventional diesel.
- Many diesel engines that can use this renewable fuel with no change in performance are already available.
- Biodiesel is also inherently cleaner than fossil-fuel diesel.

Electricity from Bio-Mass

Renewable feed stocks, such as forest and agriculture residues, landfill gases, and municipal wastes, can be used to generate electricity. Four basic methods are now being used:

- Direct firing, where biomass is burned directly;
- Co-firing, where biomass is mixed with fossil fuels;
- Biomass gasification that turns biomass into synthetic gas; and
- Anaerobic digestion that promotes biomass decay to produce methane, the principal component of the natural gas we burn today.

Electricity from coal

- Coal is the primary power-plant fuel.
- Chemical engineers have been working to provide greener options for generating electricity from coal.
- Some power plants now generate power by using coal gasification as an intermediate step instead of coal combustion, with significant environmental benefits.

Making coal greener

- Chemical engineers have made great strides to produce electricity from coal in green manner.
- They have achieved significant environmental improvements with the development of integrated combined-cycle gasification (IGCC) power plants.
- These plants generate power first by producing gas through coal gasification and then by converting the gas to power, rather than by using traditional coal combustion.
- Pollutants are lowered by this process.

Two-cycle generation

- In IGCC power plants coal is first turned into a synthetic gas.
- The synthetic gas is cleaned to remove unwanted pollutants and then burned in a gas turbine.
- The exhaust from the primary turbine is used to create steam for a secondary turbine that generates additional electricity.

ROLE OF CHEMICAL ENGINEER IN ENVIRONMENT

Chemical engineers have always been at the forefront of environmental protection. With a unique perspective that straddles both science and engineering, they work in teams with other professionals.

By designing complex solutions to our vexing environmental challenges, chemical engineers are striving to save the world we live in. One success is the conversion of the sulfur oxides in power plant gases into gypsum for use in wallboard. The removal of trace contaminants from drinking water by reverse osmosis is another.

Cars and the environmental Pollutions:

- We can breathe more easily by the contributions of chemical engineers. By designing more efficient engines that produce fewer hazardous pollutants, they have helped reduce the pollutions of cars, buses, and trucks.
- Cars, trucks, and buses are essential for transportation and freight delivery around the world. However, the exhaust from the vehicles has been a major cause of air pollution.
- Chemical engineers working with scientists and other engineers, to reduce the amount of pollution produced by engines.

Role of Catalytic converters:

The catalytic converter is one of the most important contributions to the field of air-pollution control. It is now a standard feature on vehicles everywhere. It destroys the three main pollutants found in engine exhaust.

The converter consists of a porous honeycomb ceramic base material coated with a precious metal catalyst. The honeycomb structure provides high catalyst surface area, which maximizes the contact between the catalysts and the pollutants in the hot exhaust gases.

Green manufacturing

In Because of innovations by chemical engineers, industrial facilities now capture and neutralize air pollutants before they can be discharged into the environment.

Clean water

Clean water, which is essential to human health, is also necessary for numerous manufacturing processes. Many innovative methods of treating raw water to make it suitable for drinking or for use in manufacturing have been developed by chemical engineers.

Chemical-engineering principles are used to remove harmful pollutants from both raw source water and contaminated wastewater.

Specifically, chemical engineers have developed cost-effective methods to:

- Purify water from subsurface aquifers and surface sources, such as rivers and lakes, to produce potable drinking water;
- Produce purified water that meets the increasingly strict requirements for industrial use; and
- Treat contaminated industrial and municipal wastewater and sewage to make them suitable either for discharge to public waterways or for reuse.

Chemical engineers refer to separating dangerous materials from good water as a treatment train. At various stages in the multistage treatment process, unwanted constituents are separated using:

- Vacuum or pressure filtration,
- Centrifugation,
- Membrane-based separation,
- Distillation,
- Carbon-based and zeolite-based adsorption, and
- Advanced oxidation treatments.

Recycle and reuse

One person's waste can become another person's treasure. Recycling post-consumer paper, metal, and plastic reduces the environmental impact of acquiring more raw materials. Chemical engineers help make recycling possible.

Recycling metal

Chemical engineers and metallurgists have worked together for decades to perfect metal recycling techniques.

Stainless-steel cans can often be recycled directly back into the steel mill feed stream without prior processing.

The process for recycling aluminum was developed by chemical engineers in the 1960s, and aluminum is now one of the most widely recycled materials.

Recycling paper

Paper is another post-consumer product that is now routinely recycled. Because paper mills cannot use recycled paper as a direct substitute for virgin tree pulp, chemical engineers have devised and optimized processes that involve:

- *Blending* recycled paper and water to produce a pulp slurry,
- *Removing* all inks and other performance chemicals in the paper, and
- *Filtering* the slurry to remove solid impurities.

Recycling plastics

Because plastics are used in so many aspects of our daily lives, they represent an ever-growing part of the nation's waste stream. In landfills they present a particular problem, as they do not degrade readily.

We can now recycle most plastics into useful products, because of chemical-engineering innovations. Plastics are separated by machine and reprocessed without significant material breakdown. And reuse of many such plastic products as pipe, toys, and decorations.

ROLE OF CHEMICAL ENGINEER IN MEDICAL

By deciphering the complex phenomena occurring within the human body, biomedical researchers are able to devise new therapeutic approaches to manage and treat disease.

Working alongside these researchers, chemical engineers add their unique expertise to turn many of these promising new concepts into reality. The resulting techniques and devices are now being successfully used to help lengthen and improve our lives.

Kidney dialysis

Over the past 50 years many pioneering breakthroughs in kidney dialysis have been made by chemical engineers. Often called artificial kidneys, kidney dialysis machines cleanse the blood of impurities. Since the early 1940s, when the first practical artificial kidney was developed, work has continued to create smaller, more effective, and more affordable dialysis machines.

Kidney dialysis machines represent an excellent example of the life-enhancing synergies that result when chemical engineers join forces with physicians and biomedical researchers. These “artificial kidneys” are essentially mass-transfer devices. They cleanse the blood, removing elevated levels of salts, excess fluids, and metabolic waste products. The first practical dialysis machine was developed during World War II. Since then many major developments have taken place. One of the major obstacles that had to be overcome, however, was size. To be truly practical a single-patient portable machine was needed.

Treating diabetes

The incidence of diabetes is on the rise. To control this chronic disease many patients must test glucose levels in their blood and regularly inject them with insulin. Through the combined efforts of chemical engineers, physicians, and biomedical researchers, improved techniques for monitoring blood glucose levels and administering insulin have been developed.

Recent innovations of Glucose level monitoring are,

- Micro analytical techniques that require smaller blood samples,
- Continuous glucose monitors that are implanted beneath the skin, and
- Use of implanted microchips to control insulin addition.

New advances in Insulin injections are,

- Automatic, continuous-infusion insulin injection pumps little larger than a cell phone, and
- Compact pens that combine the insulin container with the syringe.

Tissue Engineering

Tissue engineering involves the use of living cells as building materials. Engineered tissues are being created to repair or replace damaged or diseased organs and tissues. And now some of the functions performed by the human body can be augmented or replicated by this multidisciplinary technology.

Building with cells

Surgeons are able to make body wall repairs using this biocompatible material developed with the help of chemical engineers.

Promising research-and-development activities in tissue engineering involve the creation of biological substitutes used to restore, maintain, and improve tissue function.

They may even replace entire human organs. Engineered biological substitutes are currently being developed to repair or replace damaged or diseased organs and tissues.

Examples: Transplantation cells that perform specific biochemical functions, for example, improving pancreas, liver, or bladder functions;

Replacement tissues, such as artificial skin, bones, cartilage, blood vessels, tendons, and ligaments; and

Stem cells able to regenerate functional human tissues.

All these imaginative endeavors require the expertise and technical contributions of chemical engineers working in concert with biomedical researchers.

Drug Delivery:

Historically, the conventional method of delivering medications to patients has been by mouth or injection. Early advancements have included nasal sprays, dermal patches, and controlled-release products. Now, with the help of chemical engineers, targeted drug-delivery vehicles distribute medications directly to the desired location within the body and release it on demand.

Controlled and on target

- Micro medical robots, many shaped like little beetles, are designed to travel inside the body in order to treat infected areas and thus minimize the need for surgery.
- Drugs have traditionally been delivered to patients by mouth or by injection. Workings together to increase both the efficiency and safety of drug delivery, chemical and biomedical engineers have devised a variety of improved delivery techniques. These new methods also provide the added benefit of enhanced comfort and convenience for the patient.

- Early drug-delivery breakthroughs using chemical principles include: Nasal sprays that deliver finely atomized amounts of a drug via inhalation, Tran dermal patches that deliver controlled doses through the skin, and Controlled-release capsules and wafers that deliver drugs over an extended period.

Targeted delivery:

In recent years targeted drug-delivery methods have been an important area for chemical and biomedical engineers.

Novel vehicles are designed that the drug delivered to the targeted organ, tissue, or tumor.

The drug payload is then released in response to an internal or external trigger and in the amount required at the site.

Such delivery systems have the advantage of being able to,

- Reduce or delay premature degradation of a drug once it is in the body,
- Maximize the ability of a drug to travel through the body to the target site without affecting healthy tissue and organs,
- Minimize the total amount of the drug that must be administered,
- Reduce potential side effects when healthy tissue and organs are exposed to a drug.

ROLE OF CHEMICAL ENGINEER IN ELECTRONICS

The semiconductor industry was born in the late 1950s. The first microchip, or integrated circuit, was created in that period. Current generation of semiconductor chips can store 3,355 pages of text on a device approximately the size of a dime. *Chemical engineers, who contributed to the invention of semiconductor devices, are also routinely involved with the development of advanced semiconductor materials and the manufacturing processes required producing them.*

Chip materials

A semiconductor is essentially any material whose ability to conduct electricity lies between that of an insulator and that of a conductor. Germanium was the semiconductor material used in the first integrated circuit. Next, silicon was used as the base material, which led the way to the first commercial-scale production of integrated circuits.

The power behind the electronics

Turning silicon into a semiconductor chip is a detailed undertaking. It requires the multidisciplinary expertise of chemical engineers, along with many other technical specialists.

Wafers in to chip:

The process starts with the creation of a pure, mono crystalline ingot of silicon, typically 6 to 12 inches in diameter. The ingot is then sliced into ultrathin wafers, each less than $1/40^{th}$ of an inch thick.

The wafers are first polished using a specialized technique that blends nano sized abrasive particles into polishing slurry. The highly polished wafers next undergo a successive series of process steps. Each step involves the deposit of a complex layer of a conductor, a semiconductor, or an insulating material. These materials deposited in many layers produce the transistors, resistors, and capacitors that ultimately make up an integrated circuit.

Modern transistors:

30 years ago Vacuum tubes are used in radios, TVs, and early computers. Modern transistors are many times smaller than the transistors.. And the Modern Transistors many more times smaller than the Transistors. The circuits in these tiny, almost nano scale transistors are the basic tools for cell phones, iPods, computers, and so many other appliances that were not available even 20 years ago.

Making it clear

- *Even the tiniest of impurities found in process chemicals and gases can create a huge problem.*
- *Unless various engineered solutions are used to remove them, such impurities may be found in the chemicals employed during the manufacturing process. Chemical engineers are constantly pursuing advanced technologies and procedures to ensure that critical process ingredients maintain low levels of contaminants.*
- *To meet these standards, chemical engineers must specify the appropriate combination of purification techniques.*

Mass production

After the integrated circuit was first created and the appropriate materials identified, the focus shifted to the challenge of manufacturing on a commercial scale. Here, many specialized chemical-engineering disciplines, from fluid mechanics to kinetics, have been instrumental in developing current semiconductor manufacturing processes.

- *Many common chemical engineering concepts are used throughout the manufacturing process.*

- *The successful growth of silicon ingots requires an understanding of fluid mechanics, heat and mass transfer, and crystallization.*
- *During the deposition process knowledge of chemical kinetics is also necessary.*
- *It is critical to the manufacturing process that the process be carried out in an ultra clean atmosphere.*

Clean rooms:

Today's typical dime-sized semiconductor chip contains millions of microscopic transistors. A speck of dust is enough to make it useless. Semiconductor fabrication facilities, known as fabs, depend heavily on their specialized clean rooms to maintain a controlled, low level of environmental pollutants.

- *Modern clean rooms are highly engineered systems developed by chemical engineers to capture, contain, and control dust, airborne microbes, and chemical vapors.*
- *Protective clothing is worn by clean-room technicians more to protect the semiconductor devices from human contamination than the other way around.*

Ultra clean processing:

Semiconductor manufacturing facilities rely on clean rooms. The goal is to remove from these rooms even the smallest particle that could come in contact with the chips. Standards allow for no more than 1 dust particle per cubic foot of air compared with the approximately 10,000 dust particles per cubic foot found in our modern hospitals.

ROLE OF CHEMICAL ENGINEERING IN FOOD

Chemical Engineering community continues to work on advanced techniques for purifying, sterilizing, and modifying the ingredients in the foods we eat. Most food ingredients and processed foods contain unwanted contaminants, such as: Suspended solids, Dissolved salts, Metals, Bacteria, Fungi, and Other pathogens.

Chemical engineers have invented a variety of processes to remove these substances, thereby improving food quality, safety, and aesthetics.

1. <u>Membrane based Separation:</u>

- This technique uses pressure during food processing to remove unwanted impurities through a semipermeable membrane.
- Differences in size, shape, or surface charge determine what is needed and what is to be removed.
- Semipermeable membrane materials developed by chemical engineers include cellulose acetate, ceramics, and polymers.
- Numerous physical membrane configurations have been devised to separate unwanted solids and dissolved compounds from foods and beverages on a commercial scale.
- Different types of membrane-based separators use reverse osmosis, microfiltration, ultra filtration, or nano filtration systems based on the size and structure of the membrane pores.
- While numerous commercial designs are currently available, chemical engineers are constantly striving to develop even more advanced membrane-based separation systems that are more efficient, effective, and cost-effective.

<u>2. Removal of Micro Organisms:</u>

Purification of food must follow the following conditions.

- Kill microorganisms in great numbers;
- Cause no damage to meat proteins and other constituents;
- Function effectively and economically in large-scale operations; and
- Not affect food appearance, taste, texture, color, or nutritional value.

- Contamination by microorganisms is the most common cause of food-borne illnesses and spoilage.

Chemical engineers have devoted considerable effort to developing and commercializing technologies to control microorganisms such as Escherichia coli, Salmonella, and other disease-carrying pathogens. Eliminating microorganisms from meat and poultry, seafood, dairy products, grains, fruits, and vegetables helps reduce spoilage and protects consumers from food-borne illnesses.

i. <u>Traditional methods:</u>

- Traditional methods have typically been based on the use of high temperatures, chemical preservatives, or exposure to high pressures or vacuums.

ii. <u>Irradiation:</u>

- In 1997 the U.S. Food and Drug Administration first approved the use of irradiation to kill disease-causing bacteria and parasites and spoilage-causing microorganisms. Today, about 40 countries allow the irradiation of food and agricultural products.

- Chemical engineers and food scientists made this effective process. Through extensive research they discovered that low doses of ionizing radiation effectively killed disease-causing bacteria and delayed food spoilage. At the same time taste and appearance were not affected.

3. Genetic Modulations

Now with this techniques developed by chemical engineers, genetic materials can be quickly and precisely transferred from one organism to another. Plants that have been modified genetically may be used to produce crops with

- Higher nutritional content,
- Greater resistance to herbicide and pesticide damage,
- Increased resistance to disease,
- Specific desirable traits (e.g., faster ripening or delayed softening), and
- Reduced allergenicity.

Now genetically modified foods are produced using an artificial form of DNA called recombinant DNA (rDNA). In simplest terms rDNA with a positive trait is transferred into an organism lacking that trait to create the desired improvement.

Future Goals

Chemical engineers continue to work with food scientists and biotechnologists to develop more advanced techniques to transfer genetic materials from one organism to another.

Genetic modification of foods is one of the most promising and safest strategies available to increase total global food production, reduce crop losses, and increase nutritional content.

V

CHEMICAL ENGINEERING TODAY AND TOMORROW

ROLE OF COMPUTER IN CHEMICAL ENGINEERING

Definition:

Computer is a machine that can carry out routine mental tasks by performing simple operations at high speed. It has three special features which make them so useful. They are Speed, Accuracy and Memory.

Uses of Computer:

- Computer system is used to assist in the creation, modification, analysis and optimization of a design.
- It has also contributed to the advancement of numerical methods and applied mathematics.

- It is used to perform straight forward numerical calculations.
- It is also used Evaluation of expressions.

Role of Off-Line Computers:

- In a running plant, off-line simulation can gives more guidance.
- Flow sheeting of Chemical process is easily carried out by Off-Line Computers.
- Simulation can be carried out efficiently by studying the stored literature in the storage.
- The conversion of the product may be increased by relocating a recycle with the use of computers.

- Off-Line Computers of Chemical Engineering is used in Steady state, unsteady state or dynamic Simulations of *Process Simulation.*
- Conservation of Energy Resources by heat exchanging between two stream and Control of Pollution by monitoring the process was also carried out by Off-Line Computers.
- The designing of a process is guided easily by Computers.

Role of On-Line Computers:

- Interacting of digital computer and exchanging of data or information between two or more computers through wire or without is called On-Line Computers.
- In a chemical plant, a computer is connected on-line to a process, or frequently to a number of process or even a whole plant.

- On-Line Computers are mostly used in process control.
- Signals from the process are converted to Digital values.
- These Digital values are computed according to the control program and compared with the desired values.
- The results are converted back to signals to the process and maintain the desired operational level.

SOFTWARES USED IN CHEMICAL ENGINEERING

CHEMCAD:

• CHEMCAD is developed by Chemstations.

• It is an integrated suite of chemical process engineering software.

• It is a powerful and flexible chemical process simulation environment which is programmed in C++ language.

• It shows everyday chemical engineering flow sheet of the system hence product quality is increased.

• It helps to design new process and equipment.

• It helps to handle raising fuel and feed stock costs.

• Good economic comparisons by studying process alternatives.

• All engineering functions united in single software.

Aspen Plus:

• Aspen Plus is the original Process simulation software developed by Aspen Technology in 1990.

• This software is used in chemical industries for process development.

• It is a process modeling tool for conceptual design, optimation and performance monitoring for the chemical, polymer special chemical, metals and minerals and coal power industries.

Aspen HYSYS:

· Aspen HYSYS is a process modeling tool for steady state simulation and developed by Aspen Technology.

· It is used in Design and performance monitoring.

· Optimation and business planning for oil & gas production and gas processing.

· It is the only model which is used in refineries for the process like, distillation and so on.

Ariane:

· Ariane software is developed by Prosim

· It is used in utilities management and power plant optimization.

· Ariane software purpose is to reduce and manage efficiency these production costs.

· It is a decision support tool dedicated to the management of plants that produce energy under the form of utilities (steam, electricity, hot water)

BatchReactor:

· BatchReactor is a simulator dedicated to chemical reactors running in batch mode. It is developed by Prosim.

· It is designed for chemist, technicians and process engineers who need a reliable tool to reduce production cost, respond to environmental or safety regulations. · It is the detailed modeling of the reactor.

· Acceleration of scale up projects, from laboratory bench to pilot and full-scale plants.

· Cost reduction through optimation of operating conditions.

VERSATILITY OF CHEMICAL ENGINEERING

It touches every aspect of our lives:

There is hardly a single moment of the day when you are not in contact with, surrounded by, or influenced by products that are a result of chemical engineering. Just a few examples include clothing (fabric and dyes), paint, paper, plastics, soaps, cosmetics, food products, medications, and semiconductors.

It is extremely versatile:

Chemical engineering combines mathematics with the three basic physical sciences: chemistry, physics, and biology, which can be used to describe nearly all physical phenomena. Because of this versatility, chemical engineers make valuable contributions in a very broad spectrum of fields, from food processing to semiconductor fabrication and from oil refining to artificial-organ development.

It leads to many kinds of careers:

Our graduates successfully pursue a variety of paths, including full and part-time work, graduate school, and professional degrees in law, business or medicine. The innovative problem-solving skills you learn here will also help as you serve in your professions, families and communities.

It addresses today's pressing problems:

The powerful tools of chemical engineering provide leadership in attacking the most vital and challenging issues of our day, including:

- Generating energy
- Saving the environment
- Advancing biomedicine
- Developing electronics
- Enhancing food production
- Improving materials

It is challenging and rewarding:

Chemical engineers deal with exciting new problems daily and are called upon to employ innovation in creating new technologies and solving problems in existing technologies.They also receive among the highest salaries for college graduates.

OPPORTUNITES FOR CHEMICAL ENGINEERS

Research

- Many chemical engineers involve in research.
- They try to find out the best way to produce a thing on a large level, both safely and economically.
- They also try to improve existing process of all fields. If chemical engineers want to go in research field then they have to do MS/M.Tech and then Ph.D.
- After your Ph.D. either chemical engineers can do research in a university or chemical engineers can join R&D of a company.

Designing

- Interested chemical engineers will work in designing.
- Designing companies usually design a process and related equipment. They also design plants. Some of the companies include Engineers India Limited (EIL), Flour, KBR, Shel,l etc.
- Chemical engineers can join these companies after graduation.
- The companies in this field are usually MNC's so its highly probable that chemical engineers will get exposure to various countries and industries.

Production

- These companies are involved in the production of materials on large scales.

- These includes fertilizers, petroleum, pharmaceuticals, etc.
- In India There are many companies in this field like ONGC,IOCL,BPCL,HPCL,GAIL,HUL,Reliance,Tata Chemicals,RCF,Asian Paints etc.
- In abroad there are many companies like Schlumberger, BP, Chevron, Exxon, Mobil etc.
- The working condition is a little bit hard in this field as chemical engineers have to work in plant or rig etc. Usually, these are located outside of the city and sometimes even in mid of sea.
- Chemical engineers are currently working to find new sources for fuels e.g. bio-refineries, wind farms, hydrogen cells, algae factories and fusion technology. These could be applied to fuel

Space travel: Chemical engineers are currently working to find new sources for fuels e.g. bio-refineries, wind farms, hydrogen cells, algae factories and fusion technology. These could be applied to fuel space travel.

Uranium Recycler: Chemical engineers, working as uranium recyclers, will be needed to convert bomb-grade uranium from warheads into low-enriched uranium for use in nuclear power plants to ensure that the uranium shortage does not cause an energy disaster.

Genetic Pharmer: Chemical engineers are already working on producing vaccine carrying plants. Farmers of the future will not only raise livestock and agricultural crops, they will also grow plants than have been genetically engineered to grow therapeutic proteins, pharmaceuticals and chemicals. Hence they are Genetic 'Pharmers'

Nano-manufacturer: With advances in nanotechnology already offering a huge range of nanoscale processes, a new group of nano-chemical engineers will be required to manufacture these systems. This explosion of technological advances in nanotechnology will lead to opportunities arising for chemical engineers to lead the way.

Vertical Agriculture Engineer: This is one area that is happening right now. The use of vertical farms could allow us to increase food production whilst taking restrictions on land use into account. The concept of urban farms, stacked in towers or underground, with hydroponically fed crops and artificial lighting is gaining momentum. Chemical engineers would be well suited to these systems and could drastically increase our food yields and reduce further environmental damage.

Green Process Engineer: The focus of all chemical engineers is to work sustainably. Corporations and consumers worldwide are increasingly embracing green technology e.g. at the IChemE awards in November we will be celebrating achievements in sustainable technology, water management and energy efficiency.

Climate Change Reversal Engineer: As the threats and impacts of climate change increase and manifest further, a new breed of chemical engineers will be needed to help reduce and reverse the effects of climate change. They will need to be able to apply multi-disciplinary solutions to solve a range of problems.

Galactic Engineer: Galactic chemical engineers will be needed to develop processes to mine distant asteroids or planets; designing systems that can work in the extreme conditions that outer space entails. Being able to assess and then use these new materials could offer new resources, elements and materials to improve the quality of life on Earth.

PARADIGM SHIFTS IN CHEMICAL ENGINEERING

Paradigm is a set of assumptions, concepts, values, and practices that constitutes a way of viewing reality for the community that shares them, especially in an intellectual discipline.

The evolution of Chemical Engineering is guided by its following four main paradigms

- Unit operations,
- Transport phenomena,
- Product engineering and
- Sustainable Chemical Engineering.

First paradigm shifts in Chemical Engineering

- The unit operations were the first paradigm of chemical engineering.
- These knowledge have been exported to other engineering Chemical engineers proved to be a very important element in the design, construction and management of the chemistry-related plants;
- However, the first chemical engineers had great difficulties in the design, as there was a great lack of physicochemical data and in the behavior of a lot of substances.
- Mechanical and civil engineers only had done thorough studies of fluids such as air and water, but chemical engineers had to work with a huge variety of them.
- The chemist were not interested in obtaining data about kinetic constants and physicho-chemical properties, so the chemical engineers had to be put to the task of obtaining them.

Second paradigm shifts in Chemical Engineering

- Transport phenomena can be considered as the second chemical engineering paradigm, which has been exported to other engineering fields.
- Early studies and books about reactors appeared around 1940. These studies opened the chemical engineering applications and were exported to other engineering fields.
- The concept of transport phenomena leads to the knowledge that certain common phenomenaare present in the unit operations, such as momentum, heat and mass transfer.
- The study of these principles gave rise toa book that changed the study of chemical engineering Transport Phenomena by Bird, Ligthfoot& Steward.
- From the study of transport phenomena the chemical engineering texts changed their orientation becoming increasingly more mathematical, more fundamental and less oriented towards the calculation for the design of equipment.

Third paradigm shifts in Chemical Engineering.

- The study of chemical reactions, reactor design and catalysis can be considered as the Third paradigm of chemical engineering.
- This was also encouraged by the use of computers that allow programs written in floppy disks perform the necessary calculations for the design of most of the equipment used in the chemical industry.
- At the end of the 1960s, the intensive use of computers at work, the laboratory and universities transformed the education of chemical engineers, and from this transformation emerged new subjects such as:

optimization, simulation, control and analysis of processes,

- New fields could now be studied due to the computer equipment and the new books that appeared as
- Introduction to chemical engineering and computer calculations , (1976) Alan L. Myers;
- Optimization of chemical processes (1975) Holland;
- Process modeling, simulation and control for chemical engineers, by William L. Luyben (1973);
- Artificial intelligence in chemical engineering, by Thomas Quantrille (1993), and so on.
- The use of the computer for the study of chemical engineering can be considered another paradigm that was exported to other engineering careers.

Fourth paradigm shifts in Chemical Engineering.

- The approach on Sustainable Chemical Engineering is the fourth paradigm shifts in chemical engineering.

- Biotechnology is a biology-based, green engineering and is especially used in agriculture, pharmacy, food science, chemistry, chemical engineering, biochemistry, forest science and medicine.
- Biology and biotechnology were introduced in many countries to supplement the curricula of chemical engineers. In the world there are careers as food engineer, biochemical engineer, environmental engineer where biotechnologies are taught.

Many believe that chemical biotechnology can be the FifthParadigm.

Question Bank

PART-A

1. Define chemical engineering.
2. Define chemical technology.
3. List out the role of chemical engineers.
4. What is chemical process industry?
5. Mention any four greatest achievements of chemical engineering
6. Mention any four roles of chemical process industries in society.
7. Name any two famous Indian chemical engineers and mention their field which they worked?
8. Mention the role of chemical engineering in society
9. Describe the role of physics in chemical engineering.
10. What is the role of design in chemical engineering?
11. Describe the role of chemistry in chemical engineering
12. What is the role of biology in chemical engineering?
13. What is the role of design in chemical engineering?
14. Define mass transport.
15. Define heat transport.
16. Define momentum transport.
17. What is chemical kinetics?
18. State the laws of thermodynamics.
19. Define unit process.
20. Define unit operations.
21. Define batch distillation.
22. Define spray drier.
23. Give note on open pan evaporator.
24. Give note on dialysis.
25. Give short notes on agitation.

26. What is mean calcinations.
27. Describe combustion.
28. Define dehydration.
29. Define hydrolysis.

PART-B

1. Describe chemical process industries.
2. History of chemical process industries.
3. Explain the role of chemical process industries in society.
4. Explain the role of chemical engineer.
5. Explain the development of chemical engineering.
6. History of chemical engineering.
7. Explain the greatest achievements of chemical engineering.
8. Describe the greatest personalities of chemical engineering.
9. Explain the role of mathematics in chemical engineering.
10. Explain the role of chemistry in chemical engineering.
11. Explain in detail about mass transfer in chemical engineering.
12. Explain in detail about heat transfer in chemical engineering.
13. Explain in detail about chemical kinetics in chemical engineering.
14. Describe in detail about the role of process dynamics and control in chemical engineering with neat sketch.
15. Discuss in detail about the role of biology in chemical engineering.
16. Discuss in detail about the role of thermodynamics in chemical engineering.

17. Describe in detail about the role of physics in chemical engineering with neat sketch.
18. Explain the manufacturing of sulphuric acid by contact process.
19. Explain the manufacturing of soda ash.
20. Explain the flow sheet representation of chemical process.
21. Explain the evaluation steps followed in industries.

9 798887 046037

Printed by Libri Plureos GmbH in Hamburg, Germany